Vegan Diet for Weight Loss

Meal Plan with Over 75 Easy Recipes

Jennifer F. Benton

Contents

Chapter One

Introduction

Hello there,

Jennifer F. Benton Vegan, is my name.

I've been on a plant-based, raw vegan diet and lifestyle for a few years now, and I'm in love with it.

More and more people are turning to a plant-based diet, including raw veganism to varying degrees, and it's inspiring to see so many people thriving on a plant-based, vegan, raw vegan lifestyle.

By eating a diet rich in colorful fruits, vegetables, nuts, seeds, herbs, spices, and sprouts, as well as occasional treats like vegan chocolate, I've experienced big wins like improved energy, clarity, strength, mood, and high vibrations.

I sincerely hope you will find the advice in this book to be extremely useful during your raw vegan journey in the winter and throughout the year, and I would greatly appreciate hearing your thoughts.

"A Quick Guide To Going Plant-Based Raw Vegan" is another book I've written. "How To Go Vegan As Singles, Couples, Families, and Friends" and "12 Vegan Tips To Get You Started." Both are available on Amazon: "Easy Tips To Get You Started." I encourage you to add these two books to your personal library by purchasing them.

Chapter Two

If you fall into one of these categories or not, this book is for you:

Perhaps you're new to the raw vegan lifestyle and want to know how to stay healthy during the colder months.

Perhaps you're a seasoned raw vegan who wants to learn some new winter hacks.

Maybe you're an omnivore, vegetarian, pescatarian, flexitarian, plant-based, plant-forward, or somewhere in between, and you're interested in trying out the raw vegan diet and lifestyle for the first time, or learning more about it.

Perhaps you don't want to go raw vegan during the winter or at any other time of the year. My suggestions, however, will undoubtedly add to the warmth and coziness of your winter comfort, as well as your year-round comfort.

I'm writing this guide for you, wherever you are on your life's journey, in the hopes of providing you with useful information, motivation, and inspiration to help you thrive on a beautiful planet.

Even in the dead of winter, you can enjoy a delicious raw vegan diet and way of life.

It's not always the raw food that makes us feel cold, as I've discovered. It could be a lack of other practices, like the ones I recommend in this book.

Let's get this party started, shall we?

Chapter Three

THE PRIMARY INFORMATION

What Is A Raw Vegan Diet, and How Does It Work?

A raw vegan diet consists of at least 75% raw plant foods by weight. Food can be heated to a temperature of 118 degrees Fahrenheit within raw standards. Nutrients and enzymes are still preserved at these temperatures and below them. It is considered "warm-to-the-touch" when food reaches this temperature, and it is very enjoyable to eat raw vegan meals at this cozy temperature, even in the winter.

Raw vegan foods include raw fruits, vegetables, nuts, seeds, and popular foods like raw cacao and raw sprouts.

This book is for you if you want to eat completely raw or eat raw for a smaller portion of your overall diet. Whether you eat one, two, or all of your meals raw, I'll share my best tips for surviving on a raw vegan diet in the winter.

Chapter Four

Education

If you're not a raw vegan yet, or if you are but want to learn more, education is essential to thriving on this diet all year.

I recommend reading "A Quick Guide To Going Plant-Based Raw Vegan," which is a short book that I wrote. Available on Amazon, "12 Tips To Get You Started."

In this starter guide, I provide some great information, inspiration and resources to enhance your raw vegan journey.

Chapter Five

Mindset

When you decide to eat a raw vegan diet, in winter, or any other time of year, it's helpful to decide WHY you want to eat a raw vegan diet, and then remember your reason(s) front and center whenever you have the urge to say that you feel cold eating raw food, or you miss the sensation or comfort of eating cooked/hot food.

Mindset is not only key to thriving on a raw vegan diet. Mindset is also key to succeeding and achieving any goal or objective in life. There will always be times when we will feel tempted to drop our goals and take the easy, familiar and comfortable way out. These temptations can appear in many forms, including:

Of course I am not suggesting that you deprive yourself of your favorite dishes. What I am suggesting is that:

You enjoy those comfort dishes periodically.

If those comfort dishes cause indigestion, inflammation, or some other reaction, then make the decision to avoid those comfort dishes by keeping our WHY(S) in mind in order to stay on course and to continue to thrive on our high vibrations, high energy and high nutrition raw vegan diet.

Explore other ways of using the same ingredients in your comfort foods in an exciting and yummy raw vegan dish instead.

Chapter Six

Affirmations

I find affirmations to be extremely powerful in my healthy lifestyle practices. An affirmation is a short statement that allows you to channel control of your thoughts in a powerful manner. When you say or think about affirmations, they have the power to shape and create your reality.

In 2019, I met a raw vegan who said that she repeated an affirmation such as " I am raw vegan" to motivate her to stay on her raw vegan journey. I found her practice to be super powerful and I highly recommend that you consider adding similar affirmations to your raw vegan journey. For example, some affirmations that you might consider in winter and/or throughout the year, are:

I am warm and cozy as a raw vegan

It can be helpful to repeat affirmations to yourself to motivate you to stay on your raw vegan diet in winter when you find it challenging, particularly on chilly days.

By making these positive declarations an important part of your daily life, you are helping your mind to elevate and prioritize positivity instead of negativity.

Another nice aspect about affirmations is that we can use them to benefit us across our lives; not only on our raw vegan journey.

Chapter Seven

Vision Board

I find vision boards to be super powerful in achieving my goals. A vision board is a visual representation of your goals, whether in your personal or professional life, or both.

I recommend that you create your personal raw vegan winter vision board to illustrate the raw vegan winter lifestyle that you desire to experience daily.

You can create your vision board as either a:

Chapter Eight

Journal

Looking at your raw vegan winter vision board daily will be a great reminder and motivator to stay on your beautiful raw vegan journey, even when you might feel that it is challenging on certain cold days.

Here are two great articles on how to make a vision board:

One of the most powerful practices in my lifestyle is to keep a journal. In my journal I include a variety of aspects of my life, including:

What I eat and drink; and how I feel after.\s How I am feeling, physically, emotionally and energetically, in general and/or about a particular topic.

What my goals are and how I am progressing towards them.\s Etc.

I highly recommend that you consider keeping a journal to record your raw vegan journey in winter as well as your life in general as a way to become more mindful of your life and to create a deeper connection with yourself that could potentially result in many benefits for you, including becoming more aware of what you are actually doing (versus what you think you are doing and/or what you had planned to do) and where you might wish to adjust along the way.

Here are two great articles on journaling that can offer some tips for you:

18 Life-Changing Tips For Keeping A Journal
https://www.buzzfeed.com/jarrylee/life-changing-tips-for-keeping

Now Is the Time to Start Keeping a
Journal\shttps://www.nytimes.com/2020/08/29/at-home/now-is-t

Chapter Nine

Investment

As with any goal or practice in life, embarking upon a raw vegan diet, particularly in winter, requires some level of investment.

This investment can take many forms in order to thrive on a raw vegan diet, particularly in winter.

Some of the aspects of investment include:

Money to buy beautifully yummy raw vegan produce.

Time to prepare beautifully yummy raw vegan meals.

Dedication to achieve your goals to thrive on a raw vegan diet.

Research to learn about highly nutritious raw vegan food.

Equipment to assist you in preparing certain raw vegan meals.

Experimentation to discover with raw vegan foods you enjoy and thrive on.

Keeping an open mind to allow your raw vegan journey to unfold.

Chapter Ten

Trust

I have found that it is super important to practice and feel trust on my raw vegan journey, especially in winter.

What I mean by this is the following:

It is important to trust that your body will support you while you are consuming raw vegan meals.

It is important to trust that the plant foods that you are consuming are very nourishing for your body and your mind.

It is important to trust the research that shows that raw plant foods are very beneficial to your body for high hydration, high energy, high fiber, high vibrations and high nutrition.

Overall, if you doubt any of these three aspects of your raw vegan journey, especially in winter on chilly days, you are potentially sending unsupportive energy and contradicting messages to your body and your mind while consuming your raw vegan meals.

Therefore, it is very important to trust that you are making the right decision to live and thrive on a raw vegan diet, despite what others may say and despite what the weather and temperature might be on a given day.

Think

One of the most powerful tools that keeps me on a raw vegan diet, even in the chilly months of winter, is to think about how I usually feel after I eat a cooked vegan dish that includes cooked rice, or baked bread, for example.

Some of the consequences of eating cooked vegan food that I experience are:

Indigestion   Gas   Constipation   Bloating   Fatigue   Acne
Excess mucus

I think about how I usually feel after I eat a meal that includes cooked rice or baked bread, and I remember the following "low" effects that are certainly disadvantages that I have experienced when eating cooked vegan food, including:

Low hydration   Low energy   Low vibrations   Low fiber
Low nutrition

Due to these "low" unpleasant consequences, I often decide not to eat cooked vegan food. Instead I choose to eat beautifully yummy raw vegan meals (even on chilly days) that do not result in these problematic consequences.

Another way that I think about the benefits of staying on a raw vegan diet in winter, is to take the approach of "thinking forward - thinking ahead - as if looking through the front windshield of a vehicle and envisioning a wonderful life of abundance and adventure with many colorful raw and healthy plant foods.

I do not think of the raw vegan diet as a lifestyle of scarcity; of giving up cooked vegan food.

I think of the raw vegan diet as an experience of abundance; of enjoying beautifully yummy raw fruits, vegetables, nuts, seeds, herbs and spices.

In addition, I think about the "highs" - the benefits - of eating a colorful, raw vegan diet even in winter. Some of the "highs" are:

High hydration   High energy   High vibrations   High fiber
High nutrition

By thinking about your goals to stay on the "high" side of the spectrum, it will be much easier to remain on your raw vegan diet in winter even if you feel enticed to add lots of cooked vegan foods.

Chapter Eleven

Listen

Often we tend to listen to external messages, information, comments, and opinions - instead of listening to our own internal messages in our own body.

Some of the external messages we often hear when we are on a raw vegan diet are:

You need to eat cooked food for all meals.

You need to eat hot food in the winter.

Uncooked food does not warm your body.

Cooked food tastes better.

Cooked food is better for you.

In the midst of these external messages, I invite you to tap into and tune into your body. Listen to how you feel on your raw vegan journey:

Observe which practices are most effective for you to thrive on your raw vegan journey.

Lean into those practices more than other practices which you find less effective.

Each person is unique and individual in his/her body's constitution, so there will be some practices that will suit you better than others.

Chapter Twelve

I suggest that you:

Take your time.   Listen to your inner self .   Adjust your practices according to your body's comfort zone.

By listening to your body, you allow yourself to realize how good you feel on a raw vegan diet when you want to give up.

Chapter Thirteen

Compassion

If you find that you are struggling to stay on a 100 percent raw vegan diet in winter, I invite you to practice compassion for yourself. This might involve considering dropping a goal to be 100 percent raw vegan in winter and instead to consider adding some warmed or cooked ingredients and components to your diet.

Your overall happiness and health are what are the most important in my view and I wish you the very best, whether you are 100 percent raw vegan or not.

Practicing compassion for yourself is super important, not only on your raw vegan journey. It is also important on your life journey in general.

If you tend to be hard on yourself when you are finding it difficult to stay raw, perhaps this is an opportunity to also look at other areas of your life where you might be hard on yourself:

Areas where you might wish to practice more compassion for yourself and realize that life is not perfect.

We are not robots. We are not machines.

We are humans and we are allowed to adjust our lifestyle here and there to adapt to changing conditions, including - though not limited to - our raw vegan diet in winter.

Chapter Fourteen

Remember Your Why(s)

This tip to "remember your why(s)" is related in many ways to one of my earlier tips of "mindset".

When you remember your why(s) - the reason(s) you want to eat a raw vegan diet in winter - it becomes easier to keep your eyes on the "prize" of enjoying the benefits of this beautiful way of eating.

All the "highs":   High hydration   High energy   High fiber High vibrations   High nutrition

When we remember "why" we are doing something, it becomes easier to stick with it, even when it seems impossible or difficult.

Remembering your why(s) applies to all areas of your life, not only to your raw vegan diet in winter.

HEALTH

Chapter Fifteen

Blood Levels

Before starting a raw vegan diet in winter, or any time of the year, it is a good idea to understand your current health by getting a blood test to see if your blood levels are within range for your vitamins, minerals, hormones etc, including vitamin B12, vitamin D, Omega-3, zinc, and iodine, just to name a few.

For example, lack of vitamin B12 and iron deficiency can cause anemia and lead you to feel cold.

It is important to know if certain deficiencies might exist in order to avoid attributing a feeling of cold to the raw vegan diet, instead of realizing that the cold feeling could be related to a nutrient deficiency.

Here are two very important articles with more information on some recommended blood tests for vegans that will help you to keep track of your health and determine if there are any areas of deficiency.

Chapter Sixteen

Deficiencies

If your blood test shows any nutrient deficiencies, it is advisable that you consult a medical provider such as a plant-based physician, a plant-based nutritionist or a plant-based wellness coach, to identify ways to remedy those deficiencies through food, lifestyle and/or supplements.

Nowadays, there are more and more plant-based health professionals available to assist us on our vegan journey. Perhaps your health insurance provider could assist you in finding a plant-based health professional.

Or you could use one of the organizations below to find a plant-based health provider:

Chapter Seventeen

Magnesium

Magnesium helps with body temperature regulation. Magnesium is an essential mineral for staying healthy and is required for more than 300 biochemical reactions in the body.

Therefore, it is important to consume enough magnesium. Here are some raw vegan foods that are rich in magnesium:

Almonds   Avocado   Bananas   Beet greens   Cashews   Chia seeds   Kale   Mangos   Parsley   Peanut butter   Peanuts   Pumpkin seeds   Spinach   Swiss chard   Turnip

Here's a great article with more information on the importance of magnesium:

Chapter Eighteen

Calories

One of the reasons some people do not thrive on a raw vegan diet is that they are not consuming enough calories, which can have many consequences, including feeling cold.

Our calorie intake contributes to the regulation of our energy production, hormonal levels and body temperature. Therefore, when our calorie intake is too low, our body compensates by lowering our body temperature to save energy.

It has also been found that if we restrict our calorie count long term, the colder we will feel.

Here are two great articles that further explain why we get cold when we do not consume enough calories, in addition to other side effects:

Do You Feel Cold from Not Eating Enough Calories
https://www.livestrong.com/article/477122-feeling-cold-from-not-e

Chapter Nineteen

Plants for Winter

I recommend consuming organic winter plant foods that are as local as possible, including:

Fruits   Vegetables   Sprouts   Nuts   Seeds   Herbs   Spices

I prefer to mainly choose produce grown in the country in which I live (or where I am visiting) and as close to my physical location as possible, to enjoy produce that is:

Freshest/most recently picked.   Contains highest nutrient levels.   Shortest travel distance.

A part of eating seasonally involves rotating our plant food according to the seasons. In winter there is a beautiful array of colorful plant foods that are high hydration, high energy, high vibrations, high fiber and high nutrition.

In winter, root vegetables are colorfully abundant. Our bodies crave carbohydrates in cold weather so adding starchy vegetables to our diet can be super beneficial and comforting.

Some of my personal awesome winter favorites that I include in my colorful winter diet to gain the benefits of eating in season are:

Apples   Beets   Broccoli   Brussels sprouts   Carrots Cauliflower   Celery   Celery root   Grapefruits   Kale   Leeks   Lemons

Oranges   Mandarins   Parsnips   Pears   Persimmons Pomegranates   Spinach   Rutabaga   Tangerines   Turnip Plus a variety of colorful winter squash.

By rotating our plant foods seasonally, we will reap the health benefits of boosting our immune system during the winter season.

I also find that eating starchy plant foods in winter helps me to feel full longer and to stay warm. It is known that in general, foods that take longer to digest can help raise your body temperature and make you feel warmer. This is known as "thermogenesis" - the process of your body producing heat caused by food metabolizing.

Chapter Twenty

Eat The Rainbow

I believe in the approach to "eat the rainbow" which involves eating fruits and vegetables of different colors every day, whenever possible.

These beautifully vibrant colors of "eat the rainbow" are:
Reds Oranges Yellows Greens Blues Purples Whites Browns

This wide variety of colors in your diet provides an awesomely diverse combination of vitamins, minerals and phytochemicals that all nourish your body to thrive at an optimized level.

Another phrase that is commonly used to signify the same as "eat the rainbow" is "eat your colors", which is also one of my favorite phrases.

Within each color there is a unique set of healthy nutrients with their unique health benefits.

It is important to note that no one color is superior to, or better than, another color, which makes it necessary to consume a balance of all of the colors of the plant foods of fruits and vegetables.

The colored skins of fruits and vegetables are the most abundant sources of phytonutrients. As a result, it's critical to consume both the brightly colored skins and the paler flesh of fruits and vegetables.

Your meals will be:

More vibrant, interesting, nutritious, beautiful, flavorful, diverse, and aromatic

Here are two resources that can help you learn more about eating the rainbow and eating your fruits and vegetables.

colors:

Chapter Twenty-one

Obtaining Produce

There are a growing number of online options for ordering and receiving fresh produce delivered right to your door these days.

If you can't find fruits and vegetables in your local supermarkets or markets during the winter, this could be a viable option for you.

Some of your national supermarkets will almost certainly provide online delivery to your door, so you might want to consider ordering from the stores you already know.

Chapter Twenty-two

Get Rid of the Cold

One of the most common "mistakes" people make is eating raw vegan meals straight from the refrigerator or freezer, resulting in very cold produce. This, especially in the winter, can make you feel cold.

Here are a few pointers to get you started on "chilling" your raw vegan meals:

To allow your produce to reach room temperature, keep it on the kitchen counter rather than in the refrigerator or freezer when you get it home.

Before using frozen produce, allow it to thaw at room temperature for a few hours.

To remove the chill from fruits, vegetables, and herbs that have been in the refrigerator or freezer, rinse them in warm water.

Instead of using the refrigerator or freezer, keep your drinking water on the kitchen counter.

Drinks and smoothies with ice should be avoided.

Blend fruits, vegetables, and fresh herbs together to make a warming smoothie, soup, sauce, or dressing, for example.

Chapter Twenty-three

Digestion

Our body temperature rises as we digest or metabolize food, resulting in a warming sensation.

I invite you to take pleasure in the slight rise in body temperature that occurs 20-30 minutes after a meal. Because of the increased metabolic rate during the digestion process, this warming sensation can be quite pleasant, especially in the winter.

Consuming ripe fruits and vegetables to optimize my digestion process is one of the most important lessons I learned on my raw vegan journey. My digestion seemed to struggle when I ate unripe plant foods like bananas or pears.

Chapter Twenty-four

Maintain a minimalist approach (K.I.S.S.)

Keeping things simple is one of my favorite approaches to life. What I mean is that if you're feeling overwhelmed on your raw vegan winter journey for whatever reason, and you're trying to figure out how to thrive on raw plant foods, my advice is to "keep it super simple" and enjoy eating fresh fruits and vegetables in their natural state.

Eating a bowl of whole fruit, such as fresh organic apples, oranges, or pears, could be one way to achieve this.

Using a cold press juicer to extract juice from organic fruits and vegetables.

Using a blender, blend fresh organic fruits and vegetables with a little water.

Making a delicious salad with fresh lettuce leaves, tomatoes, carrots, apples, oranges, peeled and diced raw beets, cilantro leaves, avocado, lemon or lime juice, and voila!

Thank you for visiting our website, and we wish you a delicious meal.

We humans, including raw vegans, have a tendency to overcomplicate things. There will undoubtedly be times when we want to branch out from our usual routine and try something new and challenging.

There are times, however, when keeping it simple can help us achieve our goal of thriving on a healthy raw vegan winter diet.

A very straightforward approach can make a lot of sense, particularly when:

You don't have much spare time to plan and prepare meals.

I'm at a loss for new ways to make a more elaborate meal.

To make a more elaborate meal, you don't have a lot of ingredients on hand.

Bowls that are raw

Due to the obvious benefits of high hydration, high energy, high fiber, high vibration, and high nutrition, I enjoy eating large raw bowls full of a variety of raw fruits and vegetables.

If you're new to raw veganism, eating several raw fruits for a meal can be intimidating, so start small and gradually increase the amount of raw fruits you eat until you're comfortable with the fiber, flavors, textures, volume, and hydration.

Once your body and taste buds have become accustomed to eating whole fruits in large quantities (rather than drinking juices), you will most likely be much more open to the concept and possibility of eating whole fruits and vegetables.

As a result, you may begin to eat larger bowls of whole fruits and mixed salads on a more regular basis.

With time, you'll likely realize how much you enjoy these lovely plant foods and all of their benefits for:

Your gut health, your mood, your mind, your entire body, and your entire being are all influenced by your gut health.

I encourage you to include the following as the foundation of your raw vegan diet during the winter and throughout the year:

Tender baby lettuce, spinach, chervil, red and green romaine, red and green oak leaf, chard, arugula, spinach, endive, radicchio, and other heirloom lettuces

Combinations

If you don't want to eat a completely raw vegan diet in the winter, you can mix and match raw and cooked vegan ingredients to add some comfort and familiarity to your meals.

For instance, you could add the following to a salad with a base of raw leafy greens to make a cozy combination of cooked and raw ingredients:

Simmered vegetable broth. Steamed vegetables. Cooked beans or lentils. Cooked quinoa or buckwheat.

Similarly, you could make a raw vegan soup and/or raw vegan bread with some of the cooked ingredients listed above.

The flavor of life is variety.

Warming spices that improve blood circulation and thus increase body heat are another way to add warmth to your raw vegan meals without adding heat through temperature.

"Variety is the spice of life," is one of my favorite mottos, and we can certainly make life more exciting and interesting by adding a variety of spices to our meals.

These lovely, warming spices do more than just warm your body by increasing blood circulation.

Nutritional properties such as vitamins, minerals, and antioxidants contribute to dietary health benefits.

By appealing to all of your taste buds, you can add delicious flavor profiles to your meals.

By reducing repetition in your ingredient choices, you can add interest to your meals and avoid boredom and monotony.

More information on warming spices can be found in this excellent article:

Cold-Weather Spices

https://www.yourdailyvegan.com/2020/01/warm-spices-for-cold-w

Chapter Twenty-five

Powdered Food

While eating fresh, organic, seasonal plant foods is ideal, there are times when fresh seasonal options are not available.

Raw vegan organic dehydrated food powders are a staple in my diet, whether at home or on the road, for use in raw vegan organic soups, smoothies, sauces, dressings, and other dishes.

They're also fantastic in dehydrated foods like cookies, cakes, breads, pizzas, and other baked goods.

Chapter Twenty-six

Cooked Meals on Occasion

If you're having trouble sticking to a raw vegan diet in the winter (or any other season), try having a cooked meal every now and then to see how you feel.

If you're anything like me, you won't feel great and may have the following symptoms:

Inflammation, bloating, excess mucus, and acne are all symptoms of indigestion, inflammation, and bloating.

Even in the winter, these unfavorable side effects may deter people from eating a lot of cooked food.

4 p.m., raw

Some people opt for a "raw till 4" (raw until 4 p.m.) approach in the winter or throughout the year.

This way of life entails eating raw vegan food until 4 p.m., then eating a cooked meal in the evening.

In the winter or year-round, some people are drawn to a cooked meal in the evening to provide comfort and warmth.

If you feel compelled to eat a cooked meal in the evening on a regular or occasional basis, I encourage you to be compassionate with yourself.

This is, after all, your life and journey. It's not a destination; it's a journey.

There are no established guidelines.

Your journey is designed by you.

You, and only you, get to choose how you want to spend your wonderful raw vegan adventure.

Mixing Foods

On a raw vegan diet, proper food combining is especially important, especially if you have food sensitivities.

Following food combining will provide the following benefits:

Improve digestion, nutrient absorption, gut health, and detoxification.

On a raw vegan diet, you should concentrate on properly combining the following food groups:

Chapter Twenty-seven

Cookbooks

While having a large number of free raw vegan recipes accessible online is fantastic, having your own raw vegan cookbook collection is also beneficial. So, if you'd rather have your own cookbooks than rely on the internet, here are a few alternatives to consider for always having some delicious raw vegan winter recipes at your fingertips:

Chapter Twenty-eight

Catering Services

There are a number of raw vegan chefs that provide raw vegan food catering on a local or national level. If you want to try some delicious raw vegan winter recipes made by a professional, this can be an option for you to consider, depending on where you reside.

Chapter Twenty-nine

Classes

Raw vegan workshops are fantastic for learning more about the wonderful advantages and marvels of the raw vegan diet.

I strongly advise you to take raw vegan courses, either in person or online, to broaden your abilities, experience, recipes, and inspiration.

Authentic Cuisine

When you don't feel like making your own raw vegan meals at home, purchasing raw vegan local meals from a nearby restaurant might be a terrific alternative.

You may already be aware of certain local eateries or cafés that provide raw vegan choices, so these might be worth considering.

Furthermore, I recommend that you do an online search for terms such as:

"Nearby raw vegan meals"

"Raw vegan dinners in (enter your location's name here)"

If you go to a plant-based or vegan restaurant and don't see a raw vegan menu or raw vegan options, I recommend asking if they have raw vegan options and/or a raw vegan menu because it's possible they do have raw vegan options but didn't tell you about them.

This happened to me in a vegan restaurant, so I learned to inquire about raw vegan options if they exist.

Chapter Thirty

Buds of Taste

Over the years, I've developed a strategy for converting elements of cooked vegan dishes into raw vegan dishes in restaurants that are willing to comply with my request. Here are a few substitutions that I've had success with in restaurants and think you'll find useful:

Substitute lettuce leaves for the bread.

Tender greens, raw carrot sticks, and celery sticks can all be used in place of tortilla chips.

Substitute raw avocado for cooked vegan protein.

It can take time for your body to adjust to a new diet, including a raw vegan diet, and your taste buds are no exception.

Good news: your taste buds will adjust in two to three weeks. As a result, the more time you give your body - including your taste buds - to adjust, the more you'll enjoy and anticipate your raw vegan diet.

This article explains how your body adapts to a plant-based diet in a variety of ways. When switching to a raw vegan diet, you'll notice a lot of the same things.

Chapter Thirty-one

Cravings

Cravings (a strong and/or urgent desire for a particular food) can happen at any time.

Cravings or desires like these can be so strong that you abandon your raw vegan diet during the winter or other seasons.

Physical and emotional factors can both contribute to cravings.

If your cravings are caused by physical issues (such as nutrient deficiencies), you should consult a doctor.

If your cravings are emotional, you may have second thoughts about sticking to your raw vegan diet. For example, if you're craving the comfort of wonderful relationships that you don't have, you might be tempted to substitute the comfort of cooked vegan meals for the comfort of a relationship.

You can more effectively address your cravings by uncovering and identifying the reasons behind them.

I find that using the RAIN method to deal with emotional cravings and other life challenges is extremely beneficial in these situations.

The RAIN method involves mindfulness and self-compassion. I learned about this powerful practice which I use for many aspects of my life when I feel challenged.

RAIN is a wonderful tool for practicing mindfulness and self-compassion, including four steps:

Recognize what is going on.

Allow the experience to be there, just as it is.

Investigate with kindness.

Natural awareness, which comes from not identifying with the experience.

I find that once we delve into these steps and complete them with self-compassion, we often uncover the real reasons behind why we are feeling a certain emotion (such as a craving). By identifying the underlying reasons for a certain emotion(s), it is easier to address the root cause(s) and often discover ways to regulate them.

The reason I am including this tip here is so that you may consider looking a bit deeper into the cravings that might arise and allowing yourself to uncover the possible reasons that are driving the cravings, instead of abandoning your raw vegan diet immediately without really understanding what might be underneath the emotions that you are experiencing.

Chapter Thirty-two

Hydration

Adequate hydration can help you stay warmer in winter. Your body can only maintain its proper temperature when it has enough water.

Dehydration in fall or winter can cause your core body temperature to drop. Therefore, it is super important to maintain adequate levels of hydration depending on your:

Health.

Size (height and weight).

Activity level (exercise and movement).

Environmental conditions (climate: hot, cold, humid or dry).

Here are a few tips to maintain a healthy hydration level in winter:

Set a drinking goal and measure your progress throughout the day.

Consume warm water either alone or infused with a pleasant herbal tea.

Avoid alcohol consumption as it is a diuretic (meaning, it makes you urinate more often) and is therefore dehydrating.

Eat hydrating raw vegan foods such as: Cold pressed juices   Fruits   Soups   Vegetables

Limit dehydrated raw vegan foods such as: Cakes   Cookies   Crackers   Breads   Pizzas

Wear layers of breathable fabrics such as organic cotton, to minimize water loss caused by perspiration.

Incorporate adequate additional hydration based on your exercise/activity levels.

Use a humidifier to add moisture in the air, thereby improving dry, itchy skin and retention of hydration in the atmosphere.

Juicing

In my view, juicing is a wonderful mix between food and drink in the beautiful form of a hydrating food drink that consists of fruits, vegetables, and herbs. Juices can be created in either of these two options:

A mono meal by juicing only one plant food.   A combination meal of more than one plant food..

In my experience, juices have been a great entry point for me when I first started to add more fruits and vegetables to my diet. At first I was not accustomed to eating large quantities of fruits and vegetables.

Before going deep into the raw vegan diet, for me, eating fruit involved eating one or two fruits raw; or eating a cake or pastry that included fruits in the recipe.

Prior to my raw vegan journey, eating vegetables involved eating a very small salad consisting of about a handful of lettuce, a few slices of tomatoes and several tablespoons of a store-bought dressing.

So when I first started my journey to consume more high vibrational quantities of raw fruits and vegetables, I found it very difficult to fathom the concept and the possibility of eating a bowl full of about four or five fruits, or a large bowl of a mixed salad with multiple vegetables and fruits.

It dawned on me to approach the fruit topic by consuming juices so that I could benefit from the nutrition, including insoluble fiber, in the juices while not having to chew the full fruit with the visible, insoluble fiber (roughage) in its natural form.

If you are early on your raw vegan journey and/or you want to incorporate beautiful juices in your diet, I highly encourage you to consume organic, cold pressed juices either in the amount of about one or two quarts (one or two liters) per day of juices that will add many benefits to your overall health in the form of:

High hydration for your cells by extracting the living liquids from the fresh fruits, vegetables and herbs.

High energy from the power of the fresh produce.

High soluble fiber in the fresh fruits, vegetables and herbs.

High vibrations in the mood-boosting beneficial properties of the fresh produce.

High variety of ingredients, colors, aromas, textures and flavors in the different fruits, vegetables and herbs.

High nutrition in the vitamins, minerals and antioxidants in the fresh fruits, vegetables and herbs.

Deep cleansing through the purifying power of the fresh produce.

Deep detoxing through the flushing of toxins out of the body.

Deep rest for the digestive system by eliminating the body's need to digest the pulp (insoluble fiber) in the fresh produce.

Deep elimination of old waste matter from the body.

There are several options for obtaining your organic, cold-pressed juices, including:

Making your own juices at home and taking them with you to work or while traveling.

Obtaining your juices from a relative or friend who can make them for you.

Buying juices from juice shops.

Ordering juices from a juice delivery service.

Juices have also helped me tremendously to thrive on my raw vegan journey, especially while traveling. I super enjoy drinking fresh cold-pressed organic juices which can sometimes serve as an entire meal that provides highly nutritious and high vibrations hydration.

I enjoy juices that are either a single fruit or vegetable, or a beautifully yummy concoction.

If you ever feel challenged to stay on your raw vegan winter diet, then cold-presssed organic juices can be an option for you, either locally or while traveling.

There are more and more juice bars nowadays as well as juice delivery services.

In your local country you could search the internet for "cold pressed organic juices delivery" or similar phrases.

Here are a few options you might reference in the USA:

Raw Juicery https://rawjuicery.com

RollingStone article: Juice Delivery Services
https://www.rollingstone.com/product-recommendations/lifestyl

The Spruce Eats article: Juice Delivery Services
https://www.thespruceeats.com/best-juice-delivery-services-5071

If you are looking for more inspiration in the area of juicing, here are some juicing experts whom I enjoy learning from on social media:

Evie Kevish https://www.eviekevish.com

Jeff Juices https://www.jeffjuices.com

Juice Feaster https://www.instagram.com/juicefeaster

Chapter Thirty-three

Eat Your Water

There is a saying that I really like: "eat your water" which refers to eating raw vegan foods that still retain their natural water - their natural hydration - in the form of fresh fruits and vegetables.

The water in fresh fruits and vegetables contributes to keeping your body sufficiently hydrated. Eating foods that contain a high percentage of water enables you to absorb the water more slowly. This means that the water you get from fresh fruits and vegetables stays in your body longer. Plus there are the added benefits of minerals, vitamins, antioxidants and fiber, thus giving your body the nutrients it needs to be fit and healthy.

Cooking fruits and vegetables reduces the water content. It is said that raw fruits and vegetables can hydrate the body twice as effectively as a glass of water.

Here's a helpful article highlighting the fruits and vegetables with the highest water content that you might enjoy on your raw vegan journey:

Eat Your Water With These Hydration-Packed Fruits and Vegetables
https://thebeet.com/eat-your-water-with-these-hydration-packed

Liquids Must Be Consumed Take a sip of water.

I really like the saying: "Eat your liquids. Drink your solids." as it is very appropriate in describing how it is best to get the digestive process started in the mouth in liquid form by chewing your food thoroughly.

To optimize your digestion and assimilation of the nutrients in your food, it is recommended that you chew your food very well to start the digestive process by secreting enzymes in the mouth and other digestive organs of the body.

By chewing your solid food until it turns into liquid form and then swallowing it, you improve the efficacy of the digestive system. Similarly, by keeping the liquids in your mouth for a little while before swallowing, starts the digestive process and facilitates better digestion overall.

In other words:

  Chew and eat your food slowly.   Drink your liquids slowly.

This slow pace will enhance the overall eating and drinking experience by allowing your taste buds to enjoy the flavors for a longer period of time, followed by a smoother digestive process once you swallow your food and liquids.

Teas

If you like the feel of a warm cup of tea, you could enjoy a variety of warming teas that you make either from tea bags, loose leaf tea - or individual herbs and spices - steeped in a cup of warm water (not necessarily boiling hot).

I personally boil the water and then wait for the boil to subside and then a few minutes later once the water has "cooled" a bit, I make my tea so that it is "Not too hot; not too cold. Just right." as in the popular story of "Goldilocks".

Another option that I enjoy is to pour room temperature water into a mason jar and then add herbs and spices to the water and allow the plant components to infuse in the water, thereby creating a beautifully yummy and warming tea.

Here are some warming teas that will keep you nice and cozy in winter:

Ginger (freshly chopped or in dried tea form).

Cinnamon (fresh spice or in dried tea form).

Pumpkin spice (fresh spice or in dried tea form).

Spearmint (fresh herb or in dried tea form).

Turmeric (fresh spice or in dried tea form).

AMBIENCE

Hygge

Hygge (pronounced HOO-gah) is a Danish concept that refers to "finding comfort, pleasure, and warmth in simple, soothing things such as a cozy atmosphere or the feeling of friendship."

The Scandinavian term encompasses a feeling of coziness, contentment, and well-being found through cherishing the little things.

I think of hygge as an energy that feels warm and cozy due to certain practices and intentions that we have in our daily lives. I love the idea of hygge all year long (not only in winter) through many of the following practices that I enjoy:

Lighting candles   Lighting softly lit lights/lamps   Wearing fuzzy, warm vegan bedroom slippers   Wearing vegan boots lined with a fuzzy, lining   Wearing warm vegan socks Wearing a fuzzy fleece-lined scarf and hat   Wearing several layers of clothing   Adding warming herbs and spices to my raw vegan dishes for warmth   Sipping a warm cup of tea   Using warming essential oils   Layering organic cotton and/or fleece blankets on my bed/sofa   Using wooden bowls that have a warmer feeling than glass or stainless steel Using a wooden cutting board instead of plastic   Choosing wooden furniture instead of glass, metal or synthetic materials   Enjoying the warmth of a fireplace   Warm rugs/carpets

I find that these cozy details really do make a big difference in adding warmth and coziness to my environment. You might also consider including some of these elements to your personal winter environment.

Candles

I have always found candles to be a great way to add warmth and coziness to the home in winter (or throughout the year).

One of the most beautiful aspects and practices for me in northern european countries like Denmark and The Netherlands, is that, as sunlight starts to fade, they use candles to amp up the warm vibes and create a cozy atmosphere in homes, hotels and restaurants, for example.

Lighting a fire might seem like an obvious way to warm up a space. However, not all spaces can accommodate a real fireplace. As an alternative, one or two candles can brighten your space and make it feel warmer.

There are several spaces where candles can create a warm ambience, such as on your:

Bathroom counter   Bathtub rim   Desk   Kitchen counter
Dining table   Living room table   Nightstand   Patio

Since many candles include animal content (such as beeswax), it is important for us as vegans to choose cruelty-free, vegan candles, made of soy, for example.

Here is a good article to guide you when shopping for vegan candles:

Wood

Wood has a very warm feel to it and can add a cozy element to your decor. If you are going to redecorate your home or office, wood is a great option for adding warmth to a room in the form of:

Cabinets   Chairs   Doors   Flooring   Frames for paintings, posters and mirrors   Shelves   Tables   Wall paneling

Similarly, adding wooden elements to your kitchen can add a beautiful energy of warmth with:

Bowls - food bowls and serving bowls   Canisters   Cutting boards   Eating utensils   Food preparation utensils   Serving utensils   Storage containers

Plants

I super love plants. Beautiful plants are some of my all time favorite elements in my home. Not only are they lovely to look at; plants are also full of high vibrations.

Plants release moisture into the air through the process of transpiration, which is when moisture evaporates from the leaves. This can both cool and warm a room, interestingly enough. Therefore, plants are a wonderful element to add some cozy warmth to your environment while you are on your winter raw vegan diet, and year-round.

Chapter Thirty-four

Low Heat

One of the ways that you could gently warm your meals and enjoy your raw vegan diet in winter is by using a low heat on the stove (up to 118 degrees Fahrenheit or 48 degrees Celsius) for simmering meals such as soups, stews and sauces.

You could use a thermometer to measure your temperature if you wish to simmer your dish and keep it within the raw temperature range. I used an analog food thermometer while making raw vegan chocolate on the stove to determine when it was time to remove the melting chocolate at 118 degrees Fahrenheit or 48 degrees Celsius and it was super yummy.

Here's a useful article with reviews of various thermometers. Although they reference "candy thermometers", they will work great for a wide variety of raw vegan dishes also:

Bain Marie

Another way to gently warm your winter raw vegan dishes is to use a bain marie. A bain marie can be described as a hot water bath. It is used for slightly heating foods to create a gentle and uniform heat around the food.

You could put your raw vegan dishes such as soups, smoothies and sauces, in a mason jar and then place your mason jar in a bain marie for a few minutes to warm up from the heat in the surrounding water, thereby creating a cozy temperature for you to enjoy.

Here's a helpful video showing ways to use a bain marie:

How To Use Bain Marie https://youtu.be/xDllubBbdYs

Double Boiler

Another method of gently heating your raw vegan meal could be to use a double boiler.

A double boiler consists of two pots (a large one and a smaller one that nestles inside of the large pot).

By filling the large pot with an inch or two of water and setting the smaller pot (or glass bowl) on top, you can heat the bottom pot which will transfer a low heat to the contents of the smaller pot.

This can be a great option if you wish to gently warm a raw vegan dish without excessively heating it above the raw vegan temperature range of 118 degrees Fahrenheit (48 degrees Celsius).

You could warm a variety of raw vegan foods using a double boiler method, including:

Raw organic cacao   Raw vegan soup   Raw vegan sauces

Here's a helpful video showing how to use a double boiler method:

How to use a Double Boiler https://youtu.be/37UeJLo6p3Y

Sink

Another method to warm your raw vegan meals is to fill your kitchen sink with hot water and then gently place the following items in the hot water to warm them, including your:

Serving plates   Glass bowls   Mason jars

You could warm these items either with or without your raw vegan meal already in them.

Dehydrator

A popular appliance used by many raw vegans is a dehydrator. You could gently heat your raw vegan meal in a dehydrator, maximum 118 degrees Fahrenheit/48 degrees Celsius to enjoy a meal that is warm-to-the-touch.

You might also consider making a few raw vegan meals in a dehydrator, maximum 118 degrees Fahrenheit/48 degrees

Celsius, to add some variety and warmer dishes to your diet such as raw vegan:

Breads   Pizzas   Burgers   Cakes   Cookies

Chapter Thirty-five

Warm Water

One day I had some warm water left over from making tea and I decided to put a couple tablespoons of the warm water in my smoothie.

Much to my delight, I discovered that it created a lovely, warm and cozy feeling. So, I decided to add this practice as an option to my list of ways to add warmth to a raw vegan winter meal whenever you feel like adding a bit more of a warm and fuzzy feel to your meal.

You can add a few tablespoons of warm water to your raw vegan smoothie, soup, sauce or dressing to add a bit of warmth to your dish.

Hug A Mug

One of the nicest ways that I personally find to warm myself up on a chilly day is to fill a mug with warm water and to hug a mug with my hands and take in the warm and cozy sensations emanating from the heat in the mug. Have you ever tried this? I would super love to know how you felt.

In addition to the warmth of hugging a mug, the experience of drinking a warm cup of tea gives you the sensation of warming up your hands as you hold the mug and as you sip your warm tea of choice.

You could boil some water and then after it reaches a boil, let it sit for a couple minutes and then use that warm water for your tea containing your favorite herbs and spices and that way you are not using water at a super high temperature and you are still enjoying the cozy sensation of a warm drink experience.

It's like holding a hot water bottle in my hands except that it is a warm mug filled with warm water and/or a warm tea.

Plates & Cutlery

Another option to add warmth and coziness to your winter meals, without directly cooking or heating your meal, is to warm plates and cutlery/silverware in various ways including:

In your oven at the lowest temperature possible for about 10 minutes.   In your dehydrator for a few minutes at 118 degrees Fahrenheit/48 degrees Celsius.

A food heat lamp   A food strip warmer   A plate warmer A warming drawer of your stove

By then adding your raw vegan meal to the warmed plate, and/or using the gently warmed cutlery/silverware, you are benefitting from a gently warmed sensation in your meal.

Thermostat

If you are feeling a little chilly at home or at work, you could increase the thermostat temperature of your heating system (or light a fire if you have a fireplace) by a few degrees until you find your "happy place" of an optimal temperature so that you will be comfortable, even on your raw vegan diet in winter.

The reason I am including this tip is so that you consider other aspects of your environment rather than automatically attributing a chilly feeling to your raw vegan winter diet.

Sometimes it is easier to blame our diet (in this case, a raw vegan diet with uncooked foods) for certain feelings of discomfort that we are experiencing. Whereas the reason could perhaps be attributed to other elements of our lifestyle and environment, such as a chilly air temperature in our space or even outdoors.

Chapter Thirty-six

Layers

You have probably heard this tip before about how wearing layers can keep you warm, so this is a friendly reminder to add this practice to your toolkit to thrive on your raw vegan winter diet.

By wearing multiple thin layers, instead of a single thicker layer, the warm air is trapped between the layers, thereby serving as an insulator of the cozy warmth. If you remove a layer you would then reduce the amount of heat trapped which would then cool you down.

The insulating layer in keeping you warm is found to be the middle layer. Sweaters, sweatshirts, and fleece are all excellent middle layer options.

This tip is included in this guide to help you avoid blaming your cold on your raw vegan winter diet when you may simply be underdressed.

For your winter wardrobe, there are a few organic cotton thermal clothing lines that you might

pact (https://wearpact.com) is a company that makes clothing for men and women.

Extremities

Keeping your extremities warm in the winter is also a good idea because our bodies constrict the

Bedding

Using thick bedding is one of my all-time favorite ways to keep warm during the winter. You can allow your body to breathe while staying warm and cozy by layering organic cotton blankets on top of your bedding.

To stay warm and cozy in the winter, I like to wrap myself in organic cotton blankets and/or fleece bedding, including covering my head.

Throws, whether on your bed or on your sofa, are another great way to add warmth to your home. For added warmth in the winter, wrap a warm throw around your shoulders, head, and/or body.

Colors

Color Therapy, an ancient art, suggests that wearing bright, warm colors like red and copper can help you feel more warm.

For example, I chose a lovely shade of red for my winter coat, which adds to the overall warmth of my winter outfit.

Chapter Thirty-seven

Breathing

Deep breathing exercises are one of my favorite and most effective ways to get my body warm. Deep breathing exercises calm the mind and relieve stress in addition to warming the body, which are both fantastic benefits.

Breathing exercises can help you warm up from the inside out by increasing blood circulation and thus building heat in your body.

Breathing through the nose, in particular, causes the blood vessels and tiny hairs lining the inside of the nose to warm the air. Warmer air is drawn into the body as a result.

Breathing exercises that are particularly warming include:

Ujjayi breathing, Wim Hof breathing, Kapalabhati breathing, and twisting with breath are all examples of box breathing.

Two excellent articles with more information on these effective breathing techniques can be found here: Warming Up from the Inside Out with 5 Breath Practices

https://chopra.com/articles/5-breath-practices-to-warm-you-up-

Wim Hof, aka "The Iceman," on Keeping Warm This Winter https://www.sonima.com/meditation/wim-hof/

Movement

Movement (exercise) increases blood circulation, which increases body heat as your heart rate rises, causing your body to sweat (heat up) in an attempt to cool down.

When you exercise your muscles, blood vessels in your skin dilate, allowing more blood to flow to your skin. We get a warm feeling from this blood flow.

Exercising during the winter (and throughout the year) is an excellent way to:

Combat the winter blues or seasonal affective disorder by improving your mood.

Expose your skin to the sun to take advantage of the sun's role in vitamin D production.

Take advantage of the opportunity to spend time in nature and fresh air.

Exercising with others is a fantastic way to strengthen your bonds with your family. When you exercise, your heart rate rises, which alters your brain chemistry, making it easier to trust and bond with others through social pleasures like high fives, laughing, and hugging.

If the weather isn't conducive to exercising outside, there are a variety of indoor exercises that can help you improve your blood circulation, including:

Aerobics, Cross-fit, Dancing, Jogging/walking in place, Jumping rope, Pilates, Stationary bicycles, and Yoga are all examples of exercises that can be done at home.

Outdoors, there are some fantastic ways to improve blood circulation and release feel-good endorphins:

Massages

Massages, which involve applying gentle or strong pressure to the body with the hands, have a wide range of benefits.

Massages warm your body by increasing body temperature and improving blood circulation, which is the main benefit I see as it relates to thriving on a raw vegan diet in the winter.

Organic raw, unrefined, cold-pressed jojoba oil, which is very similar to the natural oils in human skin and is excellent for rehydrating dry skin.

Organic raw, unrefined, cold-pressed grapeseed oil is ideal for sensitive skin because it has a light scent and is very soothing.

Coconut oil that is organic, raw, unrefined, and cold-pressed and is extremely hydrating to the skin.

You could also add a few drops of your favorite warming organic essential oils to your massage oils for added aroma and warmth, such as:

Sweet Orange, Frankincense, and Peppermint

Chapter Thirty-eight

Coaching

There are times in life when it's a good idea to ask for help from others on your raw vegan journey, especially if they have experience coaching others to thrive in the winter and all year.

A raw vegan lifestyle coach can see perspectives that you might not be able to see because you are so "close" and "involved" in your challenges. In other words, based on your own personal background, you may have a very subjective view of how to deal with your challenges, which may be limiting in some ways.

Having an objective (neutral) viewpoint can be extremely beneficial in identifying alternatives and solutions that you might not be able to see for yourself.

I offer one-on-one and group coaching on the plant-based, vegan, and raw vegan lifestyles, and I would be delighted to accompany you on your journey with my expert advice.

You can reach out to me at the link below for raw vegan lifestyle coaching, and I hope to hear from you soon.

https://www.ayummyveganlifestyle.com/coaching/a-yummy-vega

Chapter Thirty-nine

Experiencing Cold Water

Cold water therapy and cold exposure are two terms for the same thing. While cold exposure has many benefits, one of the benefits that I see related to the raw vegan diet in winter is that cold exposure takes you out of your comfort zone and creates a resilience to the cold which is one of the biggest "challenges" that some people experience with eating raw vegan meals in the winter.

I have personally found that cold exposure (in the form of cooler shower water temperatures) has helped me to build up an increased tolerance to chilly temperatures.

There are many reported benefits of frequent cold exposure including:\s   Speeds up metabolism.

Reduces inflammation, swelling and sore muscles.

Speeds up recovering after physical exercise.

Improves sleep quality.

Improves focus ability.

Improves immune response.

By building up your tolerance to cold temperatures through methods such as cold water, it becomes less challenging to enjoy raw vegan meals in winter in that the lack of hot/cooked meals is of less importance and of less discomfort as you become accustomed to cooler temperatures.

There are several ways of practicing cold water exposure including:\s   Ice baths\s   Cold showers\s   Outdoor swimming\s   Cold water immersion therapy sessions

Chapter Forty

Fewer Clothes

One of the ways that I have built up my resistance to colder temperatures is by sometimes wearing fewer clothes in winter.

I have found that my tolerance for colder temperatures has increased by allowing myself to bundle up a little less so that my body can adjust and adapt to the cooler temperatures.

This adaptation to cooler temperatures over time is a result of the heart rate and metabolism increasing to generate heat.

Of course, I am not suggesting that you expose yourself to extremely cold temperatures with very little clothing.

I am sharing that by allowing our body to function as it is capable of doing, even in a temperature that is a few degrees outside of our comfort zone, it is remarkable how we can become more resilient to cooler temperatures, including eating raw vegan meals in winter when we have been conditioned throughout our lives to choose warm and hot meals in winter.

Here's an article that mentions a few techniques, including wearing fewer layers, as part of adapting to the cold:

Chapter Forty-one

Warm Water

Warm Water

One of my favorite practices in winter is to take a soothing shower in warm water or to bask in hot springs (as I was fortunate to experience in Iceland) (as I was fortunate to experience in Iceland).

In the summer we naturally sweat more as a result of the higher temperatures. In winter, sweating can be created by taking warm baths.

The warm water improves your circulation and elevates your body temperature, which can also help your immune system by releasing toxins through perspiration.

The steam and the warmth of the water provide a beautiful sense of coziness if you are feeling chilly.

These warming and soothing benefits from warm water can be gained by relishing in a:

Warm shower\s   Warm bath\s   Hot springs\s   Hot tub\s Steam bath\s   Steam shower

I recommend avoiding very hot temperatures in your shower or bath water as these higher temperatures tend to dry the skin which can be damaging and very uncomfortable. I let my body indicate the best temperature for me by sensing when the temperature feels "not too hot, not too cold - just right".

Here's a great article on the benefits of winter baths:

Saunas

While I was in Iceland, in temperatures below freezing, I participated in a popular practice: sitting in a sauna. It was common for people to go into the sauna and then into either a warm pool or a cold body of water while the air temperature was below freezing.

The sauna experience involves time in hot, dry rooms for a short period of time. Saunas can be an option in winter when we tend to spend less time exercising outdoors.

If you are not keen on cold exposure and building up your tolerance for cooler temperatures through cold water, for example, you might consider trying a sauna experience.

It is said that sauna use helps your body to deal with temperature acclimation (going from the cold outdoors to the warm, heated indoor spaces in our homes, offices, stores, etc.

Your body uses a lot of energy to acclimate to these high and low temperatures. The sauna helps you to train your body to acclimatize to changes in temperature more efficiently.

There are many reported benefits of taking regular saunas, as they:

- Decrease inflammation.

- Boost the immune system.

- Reduce physical stress.

Here are two articles with more details about saunas:

Chapter Forty-two

COMMUNITY

Bonding

When we're feeling cold or craving warmth, it could very well be that we are perhaps attributing these feelings to our raw vegan diet in winter, rather than considering whether there might be a lack of bonding, connections, warmth and coziness in other areas of our lives, such as our relationships.

So instead of reaching for a warm cooked vegan meal, it might be a good idea to reach out to a loved one and have a chat, either:

Virtually through a:\s   Text message\s   Phone call\s   Video chat

Or in real life with a:\s   Hug\s   Kiss\s   Cuddle\s   Other forms of intimacy

By reaching out to others and tapping into the high vibrations of a great relationship through contact with others, we can certainly add some warmth to our winter days, rather than relying on hot and warm foods to comfort us.

In other words, love can warm you up by feeling the warm and fuzzy feelings of affection between yourself and others, including nonhuman animals, resulting in a warm glow inside. By getting close to others, we feel contentment which provides a physical feeling of warmth, both emotionally and physically.

Here's a great article with more information on how love can create warmth in our lives.

Chapter Forty-three

Share

I have found that it is very helpful to share my raw vegan winter journey with others. Sharing my experience has been very powerful in helping me to thrive as a raw vegan in winter (and year-round) (and year-round).

You can share your tips for thriving on a raw vegan diet in winter with others via different portals, including:

Posting photos and/or videos of your raw vegan meals on social media\s   Writing blogs\s   Writing articles\s   Recording podcasts\s   Writing a book\s   Starting a raw vegan challenge to attract more people to join you on your raw vegan winter journey.

Follow

One of my favorite options for building community on my raw vegan diet is to follow other raw vegans on social media as a form of:

Supporting other raw vegans on their journey.\s   Learning new recipe ideas from other raw vegans.

Facebook

I have found that Facebook is a very helpful social media platform for the raw vegan community worldwide. There is a wide array of raw vegan groups on Facebook. Each group has a slightly different focus as can be seen in the title of the group.

I have personally learned a lot from these groups: from the group administrators and the members of the groups.

The administrators are great in providing factual information to the members when asked a question by a member.

On the other hand, the members share their personal raw vegan journeys. Some members are brand new to raw veganism, while others have years of experience.

It is very interesting and inspiring to see the members sharing their:

Challenges\s Questions\s Comments\s Insights\s Experiences\s Recipes\s And much more.

Some of the groups are public and others are private, so if your privacy is important to you (you do not want others outside of the group to see your comments), you might consider only joining the private groups.

Potluck

Another option that might appeal to you is to create a raw vegan potluck to gather with your raw vegan friends locally and to have the opportunity to meet new friends.

You could post your raw vegan potluck in your local raw vegan social media groups such as on Facebook, Instagram.

There is also the website Meetup where you can either search for existing raw vegan potlucks and/or create and post your own raw vegan potluck.

Meetup https://www.meetup.com/home/

Meetup

Part of the virtual world in which we live is the reality that many events are happening online only these days. Therefore, I find that Meetup is a great tool to find like-minded people in the vegan and raw vegan area of interest.

Of course there are also many in-person events happening so if that is your preference you can also attend those awesome events.

If you do not find any events that interest you, this might be a great opportunity for you to create your own events online and/or in-person.

You can find online or in-person events by going to the website:

Once you are on the main page, you can:

Type "raw vegan" in the "Search for keyword" field.

Select your location.

When I conducted a recent search for "raw vegan" there were several online events with a variety of topics such as:

"Introduction to a Raw Diet"

"Raw Vegan "cooking" mini-class"

As well as a wide variety of vegan events on many interesting topics.

TRAVEL

Festivals

It's always nice to be able to travel to a warmer location in winter. Such trips allow you to tap the "pause" button on the freezing temperatures in your hometown.

Fruit festivals are awesome events to attend for so many reasons, including:

Discovering new fruits and vegetables.   Discovering a new place/city/country.   Discovering new raw vegan gourmet dishes.

Meeting new like-minded friends.

Chapter Forty-four

Retreats

Nowadays, there are more and more raw vegan retreats organized worldwide in winter and year- round. The retreat locations are usually set in a warm climate which is awesome if you want to bask in a sunny place to alleviate the winter chill for a while.

A raw vegan retreat is a great idea if you have the desire to travel to a warmer climate while remaining on your raw vegan diet.

Going on a raw vegan retreat in winter has so many benefits, including:

Discovering a new place/country.

Meeting other like-minded raw vegan or raw vegan friendly people.

Making new friends.

Learning from the retreat experiences of the participants.

Learning about the raw vegan diet, new raw vegan (sometimes gourmet) recipes and ingredients (often exotic fruits and vegetables).

Being inspired and motivated by the retreat leaders and the participants.

Benefiting from a warm and sunny pause from the winter weather in your hometown.

Benefiting from the creation of vitamin D by your body exposed to sunlight.

Chapter Forty-five

Reread My Previous Tips

Reread My Previous Tips

There are more and more vegan hotels opening worldwide, including in tropical locations. Traveling to a vegan hotel during any season of the year is always an awesome idea.

CARE FOR YOUR SKIN

Hair & Skin

Cold temperatures and low humidity levels result in dry air that draws moisture away from the hair and skin. Harsh winter winds and dry indoor heat can make the problem worse and lead to cracked and even bleeding skin. Skin conditions such as eczema or psoriasis may also flare up during these cold, dry months.

The harsh, cold weather can strip the skin's natural protective barrier, causing water to escape (dehydration) and irritants to get in (sensitivity). The dry environment may cause itchiness which can exacerbate inflammatory skin diseases such as rosacea, eczema, ichthyosis, and psoriasis.

Some of the very thin skin and sensitive areas are the eyelids, and the skin on the lips.

Cold winter weather can also be very hard on hair by causing dehydration, dryness and breakage.

In winter, and year-round, I thoroughly enjoy massaging organic cold-pressed oils on my face, lips, hair, and body, for their overall moisturizing benefits. By massaging the oils into my body and scalp, I also benefit from improved blood circulation and stress relief by moving my circulatory system and thereby reducing stagnant energy in my body.

It's very benefit to apply organic cold-pressed raw oils on the following parts of your body in winter and year-round.:   Face   Lips   Throat   Body   Hair   Scalp   Hands including cuticles   Feet including cuticles and heels

Some of my favorite oils for retaining moisture in skin and hair are: Organic almond oil   Organic Argan oil   Organic Avocado oil   Organic Coconut oil   Organic Grapeseed oil   Organic Jojoba oil   Organic Olive oil   Organic Sunflower oil

Here are some of my favorite articles about oils for skin and hair that you might enjoy reading:

8 Best Oils for Hair Health

https://latourangelle.com/blogs/general/8-best-oils-for-hair-health

Coconut Oil for Skin

https://fleurandbee.com/blogs/news/coconut-oil-for-skin

25 Best Coconut Oil Uses

https://www.prevention.com/beauty/a20428276/coconut-oil-cures

Essential Oils

Plants have many beautiful and beneficial components, in addition to their high nutrition content. Plants also contain powerful, lovely and aromatic organic essential oils which have many awesome uses.

Essential oils are concentrated compounds in the form of oils that are extracted from tree resin and bark, roots, flowers, nuts, seeds, and leaves through processes like steam distillation and cold-pressing.

Many cultures around the world have used essential oils for centuries for various purposes including healing, wellness, and beauty.

I thoroughly enjoy using organic essential oils in winter and year-round for:

   Their aroma which I enjoy through a couple light inhales from the bottle.   Their benefits when applied topically to:

My skin (on top of a base oil such as raw organic coconut oil) mainly on my:

Forearms

Wrists

Behind my ears

My hair (a few drops for a lovely scent).

Essential oils are also awesome in other ways, including:

When added to your bath.

Applied to the soles of your feet (usually with a carrier oil such as raw organic coconut oil)   Used to create an aromatic shower steam.

Inhaled gently during yoga and meditation practice.

Inhaled lightly and/or applied topically as part of your relaxing and winding down bedtime ritual.

Inhaled gently to provide a boost during the day.

Among the many essential oils available, there are a few that you might consider using during the colder season for their warming and energizing qualities:

Ginger oil   Clove oil   Cinnamon oil   Peppermint oil Orange oil

Peppermint oil   Sandalwood oil

Note: If you have sensitive skin, it is recommended that you dilute the oil with a carrier oil like raw organic coconut oil or raw organic jojoba oil for topical use on your skin.

Here is a great article with more information on these warming essential oils: 6 Essential Oils for Winter https://chopra.com/articles/6-essential-oils-for-winter

Sleep

We all know that sleep is super important for us to thrive regardless of what our diet looks like.

The reason I am including this topic is due to the fact that on a raw vegan diet in winter we may feel that we are more likely to feel cold due to the lack of warm/hot meals.

Sleep deprivation may cause a small overall decrease in your body temperature. Therefore, it is extra important to benefit from adequate sleep so that we do not lean towards blaming the raw vegan diet for feeling cold in winter or year-round.

In addition to an adequate number of hours of sleep for your individual body, the room temperature is also important. The best bedroom temperature for sleep is approximately 65 degrees Fahrenheit (18.3 degrees Celsius). This will of course vary by a few degrees from person to person, but most doctors recommend keeping the thermostat set between 60 to 67 degrees Fahrenheit (15.6 to 19.4 degrees Celsius) for the most comfortable sleep.

Chapter Forty-six

Personal Habits of Mind

In addition to the practices that I have shared in this book, I invite you to explore creating your own personal practices that enable you to thrive on a raw vegan diet in winter and year-round.

Once you find your own personal practices, you might wish to share your helpful tips with others to assist them on their raw vegan journey.

It's always great to bring others along on this beautiful raw vegan journey and since we each have our unique perspectives, it is awesome to share our experiences that might resonate with others along the way.

Chapter Forty-seven

Reread My Previous Tips

I highly recommend that you reread my previous tips in this guide to look at which ones are easiest for you to implement on your raw vegan winter journey and throughout the year.

Once you implement the easiest tips (the low hanging fruit) you might then want to add some of the tips that might not feel so easy for you now, although you might really benefit from adding some of the more "challenging" practices that will add more warmth to your winter raw vegan experience.

Sometimes we resist adding "new" practices to our lifestyle as that requires "change" and we tend to be creatures of habit.

However, despite the "challenges" and the desire to remain in your "comfort zone", I suggest that you look at your raw vegan winter journey as:

An adventure.   An experiment.   An opportunity to try some new practices that just might pleasantly surprise you with some beautifully warming results.

About The Author Angel, also known as A Yummy Vegan, is a women's wellness coach, wellness author, and wellness speaker, helping women to thrive on a plant diet and lifestyle from head to toe.

Potluck

Another option that might appeal to you is to create a raw vegan potluck to gather with your raw vegan friends locally and to have the opportunity to meet new friends.

You could post your raw vegan potluck in your local raw vegan social media groups such as on Facebook, Instagram.

There is also the website Meetup where you can either search for existing raw vegan potlucks and/or create and post your own raw vegan potluck.

Meetup

Part of the virtual world in which we live is the reality that many events are happening online only these days. Therefore, I find that Meetup is a great tool to find like-minded people in the vegan and raw vegan area of interest.

Of course there are also many in-person events happening so if that is your preference you can also attend those awesome events.

If you do not find any events that interest you, this might be a great opportunity for you to create your own events online and/or in-person.

You can find online or in-person events by going to the website:

Meetup https://www.meetup.com

Once you are on the main page, you can:

Type "raw vegan" in the "Search for keyword" field.

Select your location.

When I conducted a recent search for "raw vegan" there were several online events with a variety of topics such as:

   "Introduction to a Raw Diet"

   "Raw Vegan "cooking" mini-class"

As well as a wide variety of vegan events on many interesting topics.

TRAVEL

Festivals

It's always nice to be able to travel to a warmer location in winter. Such trips allow you to tap the "pause" button on the freezing temperatures in your hometown.

Fruit festivals are awesome events to attend for so many reasons, including:

Discovering new fruits and vegetables.   Discovering a new place/city/country.   Discovering new raw vegan gourmet dishes.

Meeting new like-minded friends.

If you are unable to find a fruit festival in your local area, here are two awesome winter fruit festivals that might interest you for a raw vegan winter adventure:

Retreats

Nowadays, there are more and more raw vegan retreats organized worldwide in winter and year- round. The retreat locations are usually set in a warm climate which is awesome if you want to bask in a sunny place to alleviate the winter chill for a while.

A raw vegan retreat is a great idea if you have the desire to travel to a warmer climate while remaining on your raw vegan diet.

Going on a raw vegan retreat in winter has so many benefits, including:

Discovering a new place/country.

Meeting other like-minded raw vegan or raw vegan friendly people.

Making new friends.

Learning from the retreat experiences of the participants.

Learning about the raw vegan diet, new raw vegan (sometimes gourmet) recipes and ingredients (often exotic fruits and vegetables).

Being inspired and motivated by the retreat leaders and the participants.

Benefiting from a warm and sunny pause from the winter weather in your hometown.

Benefiting from the creation of vitamin D by your body exposed to sunlight.

Chapter Forty-eight

Hotels that are 100% vegan

There are more and more vegan hotels opening worldwide, including in tropical locations. Traveling to a vegan hotel during any season of the year is always an awesome idea.

Particularly in winter, a vegan hotel in a warm climate can be a fantastic way to ditch the winter chill and switch to a warmer climate where you can enjoy local, tropical fruits and vegetables.

Here are a few hotels that are either fully vegan, or they offer vegan menus, in tropical locations that you might consider for your next winter trip, while still thriving on a raw vegan diet.

I recommend letting the hotel know that you prefer raw vegan meals so that they can prepare to offer you those beautifully yummy raw vegan meals that you enjoy.

Chapter Forty-nine

CARE FOR YOUR SKIN

Hair & Skin

Cold temperatures and low humidity levels result in dry air that draws moisture away from the hair and skin. Harsh winter winds and dry indoor heat can make the problem worse and lead to cracked and even bleeding skin. Skin conditions such as eczema or psoriasis may also flare up during these cold, dry months.

The harsh, cold weather can strip the skin's natural protective barrier, causing water to escape (dehydration) and irritants to get in (sensitivity). The dry environment may cause itchiness which can exacerbate inflammatory skin diseases such as rosacea, eczema, ichthyosis, and psoriasis.

Some of the very thin skin and sensitive areas are the eyelids, and the skin on the lips.

Cold winter weather can also be very hard on hair by causing dehydration, dryness and breakage.

In winter, and year-round, I thoroughly enjoy massaging organic cold-pressed oils on my face, lips, hair, and body, for their overall moisturizing benefits. By massaging the oils into my body and scalp, I also benefit from improved blood circulation and stress relief by moving my circulatory system and thereby reducing stagnant energy in my body.

It's very benefit to apply organic cold-pressed raw oils on the following parts of your body in winter and year-round.:   Face   Lips   Throat   Body   Hair   Scalp   Hands including cuticles   Feet including cuticles and heels

Some of my favorite oils for retaining moisture in skin and hair are: Organic almond oil   Organic Argan oil   Organic Avocado oil   Organic Coconut oil   Organic Grapeseed oil   Organic Jojoba oil   Organic Olive oil   Organic Sunflower oil

Here are some of my favorite articles about oils for skin and hair that you might enjoy reading:

8 Best Oils for Hair Health
https://latourangelle.com/blogs/general/8-best-oils-for-hair-healt

Essential Oils

Plants have many beautiful and beneficial components, in addition to their high nutrition content. Plants also contain powerful, lovely and aromatic organic essential oils which have many awesome uses.

Essential oils are concentrated compounds in the form of oils that are extracted from tree resin and bark, roots, flowers, nuts, seeds, and leaves through processes like steam distillation and cold-pressing.

Many cultures around the world have used essential oils for centuries for various purposes including healing, wellness, and beauty.

I thoroughly enjoy using organic essential oils in winter and year-round for:

Their aroma which I enjoy through a couple light inhales from the bottle.   Their benefits when applied topically to: My skin (on top of a base oil such as raw organic coconut oil) mainly on my:

Forearms

Wrists

Behind my ears

My hair (a few drops for a lovely scent).

Essential oils are also awesome in other ways, including:

When added to your bath.

Applied to the soles of your feet (usually with a carrier oil such as raw organic coconut oil)   Used to create an aromatic shower steam.

Inhaled gently during yoga and meditation practice.

Inhaled lightly and/or applied topically as part of your relaxing and winding down bedtime ritual.

Inhaled gently to provide a boost during the day.

Among the many essential oils available, there are a few that you might consider using during the colder season for their warming and energizing qualities:

Ginger oil   Clove oil   Cinnamon oil   Peppermint oil
Orange oil

Peppermint oil   Sandalwood oil

Note: If you have sensitive skin, it is recommended that you dilute the oil with a carrier oil like raw organic coconut oil or raw organic jojoba oil for topical use on your skin.

Here is a great article with more information on these warming essential oils: 6 Essential Oils for Winter https://chopra.com/articles/6-essential-oils-for-winter

Chapter Fifty

CONCLUSION

Personal Habits of Mind

In addition to the practices that I have shared in this book, I invite you to explore creating your own personal practices that enable you to thrive on a raw vegan diet in winter and year-round.

Once you find your own personal practices, you might wish to share your helpful tips with others to assist them on their raw vegan journey.

It's always great to bring others along on this beautiful raw vegan journey and since we each have our unique perspectives, it is awesome to share our experiences that might resonate with others along the way.

CPSIA information can be obtained
at www.ICGtesting.com
Printed in the USA
LVHW060116010422
714790LV00007BA/439